SCHIRMER'S LIBRARY
OF MUSICAL CLASSICS

Anthology of Italian Song
Of the Seventeenth and Eighteenth Centuries

Selected and Edited with Biographical Notices by

ALESSANDRO PARISOTTI

English Translations by

DR. THEODORE BAKER

BONONCINI	MARCELLO
CALDARA	MARTINI
CARISSIMI	PAISIELLO
CESTI	PERGOLESI
GLUCK	PICCINNI
HANDEL	A. SCARLATTI
JOMELLI	D. SCARLATTI
LEGRENZI	TRAETTA
LOTTI	VIVALDI

Book I . . . . . Library Vol. 290

Book II . . . . . Library Vol. 291

G. SCHIRMER, Inc., NEW YORK

PREFACE.

WHILE in all art a loving investigation of ancient forms is an unfailing bourn whence flow the most fitting resources for the purification of taste, this applies most fully to music, which, eluding plastic realism, can readily derive from grand models whatever it may need for the improvement and development of its productions. This assertion appears like, and in fact is, a paraphrase of the well-known saying of our great modern melodramatist, the sense of which may perhaps be more directly and forcibly felt in the original general form. And since the new is now-a-days growing scarcer and scarcer, its place may fortunately be filled by the resurrection of the ancient ; the more, because it has appeared for some time as if such a resurrection would interest patrons of art far more than current novelties. For these two reasons, then, the time seemed to be ripe for the present publication ; and it cannot fail to be a source of real benefit to our beloved art of song, to point out a means for certain improvement both on the æsthetic and practical side. The songs which follow were gleaned from old manuscripts and ancient editions, where they lay in unmerited oblivion. In undertaking this work of exhumation, such an abundance of material was unearthed that the task of rejection, necessitated by the modest proportions of this volume, became difficult and grievous. [Since the above was penned, the very favorable reception accorded to this first volume has encouraged the preparation and publication of a second.] In transcribing the melodies the utmost care was taken to alter nothing in the originals, and often various manuscripts were consulted to ascertain the most elegant and correct form. Obsolete abbreviations were written out in full, and the melodies so selected that none overstep the range of an ordinary voice, thus making them accessible to all. Further, in adding the accompaniments and harmonizing the *bassi continui*, care was taken to insert nothing out of keeping with the words or character of the compositions, or with the style of the author and his period; during this work constant reference was made to the models left by the greatest masters in this style of chamber-music, placed in centuries past at the lofty elevation which is theirs of right.

Having explained the scope of this publication, a few observations on the correct mode of interpreting the music will be offered. The main characteristics peculiar to the composers of the 17th and 18th centuries are clearness and simplicity of form, depth of feeling, and a suave serenity whose grateful influence permeates their entire style. The music of to-day, on the contrary, is neurotic, full of startling effects and violent contrasts. In the interpretation of these ancient songs, therefore, a prime requisite is the avoidance of any exaggeration of *coloris,* of all strained delivery. The singing must be simple, unaffected, tranquil, *legato ;* the *tempi* quiet, without any precipitation whatever ; the embellishments executed with studious attention, to insure clearness and accuracy ; words and tones welded to form one indissoluble whole, so that the hearer cannot fail to comprehend their meaning. The whole delivery; in short, should show delicacy of intuition and a thorough understanding of the laws of the good Italian style ; it should be at once calm, elegant, correct, and expressive, yet without coldness or heaviness. No unusual powers are required for singing these ancient songs, though they demand an exact observance of the notes and directions ; a modicum of good taste, and a genuine love of study, will do the rest.

Rome. November, 1885.

BIOGRAPHIES OF AUTHORS REPRESENTED IN THIS COLLECTION.

GIOVANNI MARIA BONONCINI.
1640–1678.

BY exploring the libraries not a few of Bononcini's works, distinguished by elegance of form and exquisite taste, may be brought to light. Madrigals, symphonies, cantatas and sonatas form a rich and attractive repertory, well worthy of being recalled to life through the agency of the press. But matters are not yet ripe for taking this step, and we must be satisfied if a small portion of these delightful compositions meets with universal approval ; albeit the style of Bononcini is clear, melodious, and unspeakably expressive. In each measure wells up the art of beautiful song ; at every turn are effects surprising in their freshness and aptness.

The arietta printed here was found in an old manuscript of the 18th century, stowed away amidst other gems of the most illustrious Italian composers, in the great library of the Royal Academy of St. Cecilia at Rome. After this manuscript Gavaert edited, in the collection entitled *Gloires d'Italie*, a pleasing melody, "Pietà mio caro bene," which I should have been glad to add to the present series had space not been lacking. Unerringly correct in form, graceful in style, most truthful in the expression of feeling, Bononcini the Modenese, besides being a most eminent composer, was a famous teacher. This is plainly proved by his work, "Il musico pratico" (The practical musician), "a brief demonstration of the manner of attaining a complete knowledge of all those things which belong to the composition of songs and which concern the art of counterpoint," published in 1673.

He wrote theatrical works, instrumental pieces, secular sonatas, madrigals, and some cantatas.

He was born about 1640, and died November 19, 1678.

ANTONIO CALDARA.
1670–1736.

HE was master of composition to Charles VI, at whose court in Vienna he bore the title of Capellmeister. Previously, he had occupied a similar position at the ducal court in Mantua. An extremely fruitful writer, he left to posterity a long list of sacred and secular works, in all of which the trained hand of the master in art is apparent. The simple and affecting melody, "Come raggio di sol," has lost nothing of its original delicacy and freshness after the lapse of two centuries. Among the numerous cantatas and serenatas from his pen, the pastoral drama entitled *La costanza in amor vince l'inganno* appears peculiarly worthy of mention. Its plot is simple and perfectly idyllic, but the graces of song are lavished throughout with a prodigal hand. He rarely mentions the instruments for the accompaniment, excepting where he writes an *obbligato* for theorbo, *corno da caccia*, the treble viol, etc. In most cases, there is a bare *basso continuo* set underneath the vocal part, with no indication whatever of the harmonization. From the above-mentioned drama we have selected the two ariettas, "Sebben crudele" and "Selve amiche," and should have taken more had space permitted.

Caldara was a pupil of Legrenzi, and enjoyed a higher reputation than his teacher

He set to music libretti by Apostolo Zeno and Pietro Metastasio, among them being *Temistocle*. He was born at Venice in 1670, and died in the same city in 1763.

GIAN GIACOMO CARISSIMI.

1604(?)–1674.

A MORE fitting commencement for this Collection of Ancient Music could hardly be found than a work by a genius of such rare and original type as Carissimi; who, among the great masters of the 17th century, was famous both as a composer and as a teacher of singing. His *Sacrifice of Jephtha* and *Judgment of Solomon*, master-works of the sacred style, founded the grand Italian school continued and extended with such admirable success by his pupils Alessandro Scarlatti and Marco Antonio Cesti. It is much to be regretted that the majority of this fertile author's compositions lie neglected, as dusty and decaying manuscripts, in public libraries, which, possessed of treasures in the shape of scientific and literary works, regard musical writings as poor appendages of slight worth. Hence the difficulty of researches, which might reveal to lovers of art many a hidden treasure and gem of price.

Carissimi, in his life as an artist, was very retiring, and it is not known whether his ppointment to the directorship of the choir in S. Appollinare at Rome brought him greater honor than that at Assisi. However this may be, to his eminent genius and unwearying study of music is due a great advance in musical art, more especially in the style of oratorio and songs.

From among these latter we have selected for publication the one set to the words, *Vittoria, vittoria*. A poor lover has liberated himself from love's bondage, which appears to have been very grievous, and expresses his delight with the most charming vivacity, and in the most elegant form. This song has a character of such marked individuality, that it would be difficult to confound it with other similar compositions.

Carissimi was born at Marino, near Rome, about the year 1604, and died in Rome in 1674. Some biographers contend that he was born at Venice in 1582.

MARCO ANTONIO CESTI.

1620–1669 (?).

AMONG the followers of Carissimi was the monk Fra Marc'Antonio da Arezzo, who was born in that city about 1620, and died at Venice in 1669, or according to others at Rome in 1688. He was a pupil of Carissimi, and one of the foremost composers of the 17th century. His cowl did not hinder him from writing various dramas and amorous cantatas in the style originated by Carissimi, in which aria and recitative alternate, besides many madrigals and secular ariettas.

Not a few of this composer's manuscripts are left us, scattered everywhere through the libraries, and generally neglected. From among these I have been able to select, in the library of the Royal Academy of St. Cecilia and the Chigiana at Rome, a few little songs for three voices with romantic or mythological subjects, and of no mean value, which I hope to see published sooner or later. Cesti's style is wonderfully suave and melodious, and expressive to a degree that might be called sensuous. These features are strongly prominent in the melody "Intorno all' idol mio" belonging to the opera *Orontea*, which was performed in 1649; it may also be found in the fine collection of Carl Banck, entitled *Arien und Gesänge älterer Tonmeister* (Arias and Songs by Earlier Composers).

Numerous other melodies in this author's secular music, with *basso continuo*, deserve to be brought to light, both by reason of their interesting melodic turn and the elegance of their form; and I propose having them printed in case this first attempt should meet with critical and popular approval.

Cesti was *maestro di cappella* at Florence under Ferdinando III de'Medici, and later assistant Capellmeister to Leopold I at Vienna. His most successful work was the opera *La Dori;* the titles of ten or twelve others are still extant.

CHRISTOPH WILIBALD GLUCK.

1714–1787.

IT is with good reason that Gluck is called the reformer of the musical drama; for during the better part of his long career as an artist he devoted all the exceptional powers of his genius to the emancipation of the opera from the shackles of conventional form. In his efforts he met with a redoubtable rival in Piccinni, of whom we shall speak later; so hot was their struggle for supremacy at the French court, that two opposing parties were formed, the Gluckists and the Piccinnists—a striking proof of the interest then taken in art by the public. Piccinni was finally defeated by the immense success attending the performance of Gluck's opera *Iphigenia in Tauris.* The principle at issue in this artistic war was, whether natural dramatic expression in music, as advocated by Lully and Rameau and practically carried out by Gluck, should give way to the mere outward charm of lyrical melody as demanded by the Italian school of singers. Gluck's later operas are masterpieces of true dramatic effect, and the grander the situations, the more boldly does his genius assert itself. At the beginning, however, he was satisfied to follow in the footsteps of the early Italian composers; not until the fiasco of his operas in London (1746) did he seriously address himself to that reformation of his own style which was destined to work a revolution in dramatic music. As a French writer of the time happily put it, "the Italian opera was only a concert for which the drama furnished the pretext." In Gluck's operas, on the other hand, his devotion to truth in dramatic art breathes from every page.

Gluck was born at Weidenwang in the Upper Palatinate on July 25, 1714, studied in Komotow, Prague, Vienna and Milan, in which last-named place his first operas, with Italian words and in the Italian style, were brought out; their success earned him an invitation to London, where the fiasco above alluded to led to the change in his views, which was confirmed by a visit to Paris, where he heard Rameau's operas. The operas, *Alceste* and *Paride ed Elena,* were performed at Vienna in 1767 and 1769 respectively; from the latter is taken the aria "O del mio dolce ardor," in which suave melody, elegance of form, and exquisite dramatic feeling unite to form a rea gem of art. Despite the incontestable beauties of these works, they met with little favor in Vienna; their author consequently removed to Paris, where fame and fortune were the meed of his unwearied efforts He died at Vienna November 15, 1787.

GEORGE FREDERICK HANDEL.

1685–1759.

HANDEL (properly Georg Friedrich Händel) was born at Halle in Germany on the 23d of February, 1685, not quite a month before Joh. Seb. Bach. His precocious genius attracted the attention of the Duke of Saxe-Weissenfels, who prevailed on his father to provide for his regular instruction in music. At the age of ten he had written a series of sonatas, and in the following year his father journeyed with the youthful composer to Berlin, where his talent for improvisation and playing from a figured bass aroused the admiration of the Italians Bononcini and Ariosti. In 1702 he was appointed organist of the cathedral at Halle, a position which he retained only a year, then going to Hamburg, where his first four operas (in German) were written, *Almira* being especially successful. In 1706 he journeyed to Italy, the home of the opera, and spent over three years in Florence, Rome, and Venice, studying diligently and composing several operas and oratorios in Italian. Thoroughly at home in the Italian vocal style, and already noted as a composer, he came to London in 1710, where he was received with marked distinction; nearly thirty Italian operas written during the ensuing twenty-five years spread his fame far and wide. The opera *Ottone*, from which the arietta "Affanni del pensier" is taken, appeared in 1725; *Alcina*, containing "Ah mio cor, schernito sei," in 1736. Various oratorios, among them *Esther* and *Acis e Galathea*, had also been brought out in the meantime, and met with much favor; besides, Handel had his hands full as a conductor and opera-manager; yet he found time to compose a great number of valuable instrumental works, and made several trips to the continent in search of singers and orchestra-players. His first unquestioned success in oratorio was with the *Messiah*, written in 1741 in twenty-four days; thenceforward he occupied himself almost exclusively with this style of composition, and produced the masterworks which render his fame imperishable. He died at London in 1759, honored and revered in the country of his adoption as no musician before him.

NICCOLA JOMMELLI.

1714–1774.

A PROLIFIC composer in a style peculiarly his own, Niccola Jommelli, one of the foremost opera-writers of the Neapolitan school, was born at Aversa, near Caserta, the 10th of September, 1714, and died at Naples August 25th, 1774. In the last-named city he studied under Durante, Leo, and Mancini, and at Bologna under P. Martini. His name is still a household word in Italy; indeed, on reading any of his compositions, one cannot fail to recognize the stamp of a great genius and of true originality There is something out of the common in Jommelli's music, captivating the hearer by its breadth of conception and the careful working-out of details. At times excessively minutiose, he introduces the flourishes so admired at that period with a lavish hand, as in the celebrated motet *Victimæ paschali*, which, if not the greatest, is certainly one of the most perfect of his works. At all events, he always avoided crudities, and, by combining the charm of novelty with grace of form, has created real works of art. An experience of fourteen years (1754–1768) as Royal Music-Director at Stuttgart, wrought a marked change in his style, which won the applause of the Germans, but which was so little to the taste of the Italians that on his return to Naples his three last —and perhaps best—operas were totally unsuccessful. Jommelli took this cold reception so much to heart, that his death soon followed; his last work was the celebrated *Miserere* for two soprani and orchestra.

He wrote not only operas, but also oratorios, melodramas, masses, motets, requiems, psalms for double chorus, etc. His earlier successes were doubtless due in part to the coöperation of Metastasio, the renowned writer of opera-libretti, concerning whom the following interesting remarks are found in some of Jommelli's letters: "He is a round, fat man of pacific disposition and engaging mien, and with very quiet and elegant manners."—"He is the cleverest artist in adapting music to words of all that I have ever known. If you should ever happen to make his acquaintance, you will be sure to like him; he is certainly the most amiable glutton that ever lived."

GIOVANNI LEGRENZI.
1625–1690.

OF this composer who was born at Clusone near Bergamo in 1625, and died at Venice, where he was *maestro di cappella* in San Marco, in 1690, seventeen theatrical works, and numerous masses, motets and psalms, concertos, sonatas, and cantatas are extant. He was one of the first to write trios for two violins and 'cello, and enjoyed the reputation of being one of the best composers of the 17th century. He was the director of the ducal musicians at Ferrara, and of the Conservatorio de'Mendicanti at Venice; he considerably enlarged the orchestra of St. Mark's, raising the number of players to thirty-four (eight violins, eleven small viols, two tenor viols, three viole da gamba and contrabass viols, four theorbos, two cornetti, one bassoon, and three trombones). The selected arietta "Che fiero costume," taken from the opera *Etocle*, and effeminate like nearly all the poetry of the period, lacks neither freshness nor boldness, qualities on which changes of fashion have no hold. Its effect is charming, and the style chaste throughout. It therefore appears to me not to be out of place in this collection. Pupils of Legrenzi were Antonio Caldera and Antonio Lotti. It is claimed by some that he wore priestly vestments.

ANTONIO LOTTI.
1667–1740.

A PUPIL of Giovanni Legrenzi, and his successor as music-director at San Marco in Venice, Lotti was an eminent composer of sacred music and operas; his first opera, *Giustino*, was brought out at Venice when he was but sixteen years of age. An expert in the art of handling the voice, which was his favorite department of music, he founded a celebrated school of singing at Venice. Among his pupils were Benedetto Marcello, Galuppi (Buranello), and other fine musicians. He outstripped his teacher not only in fertility of invention, but in beauty or form and the expression of emotion, and ranks among the foremost original artists of the time. In the arietta "Pur dicesti, o bocca bella," simplicity, clearness, and infinite grace are so happily combined, as still to challenge our admiration.

His knowledge of the art of singing is apparent throughout this composition, and particularly in the effects of the portamento and syncopation, the elegant style, and a wise economy in the management of coloratura and embellishments. Some biographers assert that Lotti was born at Hanover in 1667, of Venetian parents, his father being music-director at the Electoral Court; others say that he was born at Venice in 1665; he died at Venice January 5, 1740.

BENEDETTO MARCELLO.
1686–1739.

THE work "Estro poetico-armonica," better known now-a-days under the title of Psalms of Marcello, rendered its author famous among his contemporaries, and secured the admiration of posterity. He was a *littérateur* and poet of considerable merit, and wrote a *Treatise on musical theory according to modern practice*, the *Teatro alla moda*, a poem, *Arato in Sparta*, and other literary works. In his capacity as a musician he composed oratorios, cantatas, serenatas, masses, motets, etc., written in a severe style, but filled with the inspiration of true genius. The arietta "Quella fiamma che m'accende" is characterized by its smooth and tasteful style; its harmony has a graceful and original turn, and the general effect is excellent. In Banck's Collection it is quoted several times.

Benedetto Marcello was a pupil of Lotti, a sketch of whom is given above, and o Francesco Gasparini of Lucca. He was born at Venice of noble family, on August the 1st, 1686; studied law, becoming a barrister, and for fourteen years was one of the council of Forty; removed to Pola, where he held the post of *provveditore* for eight years, contracting in that fatal climate the germs of a malady which ended his life in 1739. He secretly married a girl of obscure origin, one of his pupils, having fallen desperately in love with her. In the church of San Giuseppe dei Franciscani at Brescia the following inscription may be found on his tomb:

BENEDICTO MARCELLO
SCIENTISSIMO PHILOLOGO
POETÆ
MUSICES PRINCIPI.

GIOVANNI MARTINI.

1741–1816.

THE lovely melody "Piacer d'amor" has frequently been attributed to the celebrated Padre Martini (Giambattista Martini), the author of the *Storia della musica;* but the most careful editors, among them Banck in his Collection, have cast doubts upon his authorship, and it would now appear settled that its writer was Jean Paul Egide Schwarzendorf, who was born at Freistadt in the Palatinate, and, on removing to Nancy in 1760, Italianized his name, in accordance with a fashion not yet obsolete. His career was replete with curious adventures. At the age of ten he became organist of the Jesuit seminary at Neuburg, where he was inscribed as a student; seven years later we find him organist in the Franciscan church at Freiburg, where he decided to devote himself wholly to music. Not knowing whither to betake himself, he resorted to the expedient of ascending a high tower, from the top of which he let fall a feather; as the feather drifted towards France, he started for Nancy, without a penny in his pocket. On the way he found shelter in various cloisters, in which his skill as an organist won him favorable attention. In Nancy he obtained a situation in the workshops of the organ-builder Dupont, who, recognizing his genius, generously aided him. He changed his name, as mentioned above, and became a music-teacher (1760); four years later he proceeded to Paris, where his success in a competitive composition of a march earned him high protection, through which he was appointed officer *à la suite* of a cavalry regiment, the leisure thus obtained being at first employed in writing military music. In 1771, however, he composed an opera entitled *L'amoureux de quinze ans,* a work marking the beginning of a brilliant career. He became noted and popular under the name of Martini the German; the Prince of Condé made him his *maître de chapelle,* a post exchanged later for a similar one under the Count of Artois; after the vicissitudes of the Revolution, he finally secured the position of Intendant of the Conservatory. He died at Paris in 1816.

A talented composer and distinguished harmonist, he wrote twelve operas, various masses, requiems, psalms and other sacred compositions, six quartets for flute with string trio, twelve trios for two violins with 'cello, etc., etc., besides numerous instruction-books. Fétis says of him: "His melodies were expressive and dramatic; his romances, preceding those of Garat and Boieldieu, may be regarded as models of their kind, and that which he wrote on the words *Plaisir d'amour* will always be quoted as a *chef d'œuvre* of grace and gentle melancholy."

GIOVANNI PAISIELLO.

1741–1816.

PAISIELLO was one of the brightest stars of the 18th century; eminent as a composer of opera, and especially so as a writer of *opera buffa,* he also tried his hand at nearly every other style of musical composition, and in all was both elegant and powerful, simple, yet original. From his native town of Taranto, where he was born Mav

9, 1741, he went to Naples, studying there for five years as a pupil of Durante, when he received an appointment as assistant teacher at the Conservatorio Sant' Onofrio; the immense success of a comic intermezzo written by him, and performed in the theatre of the Conservatory, brought in its train a host of orders from the theatres. Nearly one hundred operas were the fruit of his artistic career, which from beginning to end was a series of almost uninterrupted triumphs. His musical setting of "The Barber of Seville" enjoyed such extraordinary popularity, that when Rossini ventured to compose the same subject there were not a few who prophesied his failure. Among his best operas may be mentioned *La bella Molinara, Gli Zingari in fiera,* and *Nina pazza per amore,* from the first of which the arietta "Nel cor più non mi sento," from the second the canzone "Chi vuol la zingarella," and from the third the aria "Il mio ben," are taken. The genuine musical value of these little gems will sufficiently recommend them to all lovers of *il bel canto.*

Like so many of the leading Italian musicians of the period, Paisiello spent a considerable portion of his life in foreign lands, chiefly in Paris and St. Petersburg; at the time of his decease he held the position of Director of the Conservatory at Naples.

GIOVANNI BATTISTA PERGOLESI.

1710–1736.

WHO could read unmoved the touching story of the death of this swan of Jesi? His career, unlike that of so many Italian composers of the time, whose works were during their lives lauded to the skies, only to meet with oblivion after their death, was a series of bitter disappointments; not until he had passed away did his compositions find the recognition they deserved. He was born at Jesi, January 4, 1710, and at a very early age was admitted to the Conservatorio dei Poveri at Naples; his original improvisations on the violin attracted attention, and secured him careful instruction from such teachers as Durante and Francesco Feo; far from adopting their style, however, he formed one of his own, in which melody and expression were not sacrificed to contrapuntal science. His last school-work, a sacred drama entitled "The Conversion of San Guglielmo," performed with comical intermezzi at the cloister of San Agnello, and also his two first operas of the same year, appear to have had little success; but a series of trios written for a princely and intelligent patron paved the way to a commission from the king to write a solemn mass dedicated to the patron saint of Naples, on occasion of a violent earthquake; the favorable reception of this mass encouraged further attempts in the same line, which made his name known in that city, at least. His most celebrated operetta, or rather intermezzo, *La serva padrona,* was written in 1731, but despite the delightful freshness of the music and the novelty (at that time) of the plot, it made scarcely any impression; several other operas brought out in succession met with a similar fate. The indifference shown to his compositions, a weak constitution, and (it is said) an unhappy love-affair, combined to undermine his health to such an extent that he was forced to seek relief in the sea-baths of Pozzuoli; but his strength was too far exhausted, and death terminated his woes on April the 17th, 1736. The last work from his pen was the justly renowned *Stabat mater,* which he finished on his death-bed, and for which he received the munificent remuneration of ten ducats (42½ florins).

The arietta "Stizzoso, mio stizzoso," from *La serva padrona,* bears the stamp of original genius in its graceful, sparkling melody and admirable comic effect, and is a fine specimen of the naturalness and originality of Pergolesi's style.

NICCOLO PICCINNI.
1728–1800.

THIS celebrated rival of Gluck, already mentioned in the sketch of the latter, was born at Bari in 1728; a stroke of paralysis caused his death at Passy, in 1800. The aria selected for publication is taken from the opera *Le faux Lord*, and is well calculated to show the genius of its author. The freshness of the melodic movement and the discreet use of harmonic resources render it difficult to believe that the music was actually written more than a century ago. Admitting that Gluck, his successful rival, was a master in orchestral color and strong dramatic passion, Piccinni was assuredly no less great in harmonic resources and in the true expression of the tenderest emotion. He was one of the most prolific opera-composers who have ever lived; he wrote over one hundred and fifty dramatic works, which were extremely popular both in France and Italy. A pupil of Leo and Durante, he followed faithfully in their footsteps, merely broadening, as the progress of art required, the horizon of the melodic and instrumental forms. His kindly and genial nature neither allowed him to take part in the intrigues at the French court, where his adherents endeavored to compass Gluck's downfall, nor to feel any bitterness at the success of his competitor for the public favor. And later in life, when death had removed his redoubtable rival Sacchini from the court of Vienna, Piccinni held, at the funeral, a discourse full of the most generous praise for the eminent composer. He has been called the father of *opera buffa*, a titled merited, in particular, by reason of the exquisite construction of all his works in that style. Though high in favor at the court of Marie Antoinette, the difficulties which he naturally encountered in setting a foreign language to music would seem to account, at least in part, for his ultimate ill-success. His most unfortunate venture was, undoubtedly, the attempt to compose *Iphigenia in Tauris,* in opposition to Gluck's masterpiece; which latter finally drove Piccinni from the field.

ALESSANDRO SCARLATTI.
1659–1725.

POTENT in artistic conception, of most fertile and versatile genius, Alessandro Scarlatti, the illustrious founder of the Neapolitan school, was not only a great composer, but equally great as a singer and as a player on the harp and harpsichord. Himself the pupil of Carissimi, his own most celebrated pupils were Leo, Pergolesi, and Durante, to whom he bequeathed an innumerable host of masses (200), operas (106), oratorios, cantatas, madrigals, motets, toccatas, serenades, etc. He was *maestro di cappella* at the Neapolitan court, and later at the cathedral of Santa Maria Maggiore in Rome; afterwards returning to Naples, where he also acted as Director of a conservatory. In his compositions a flowing style is united with elegance, yet simplicity, of form. He was the first to introduce the *da capo* into the grand aria (in his opera *Teodora*, brought out at Rome in 1693). Most of his compositions are written over a *basso continuo* with or without figures, and his style is always correct, simple, and expressive. Though the modulations are somewhat bold for his period, clearness never suffers thereby. He was born at Trapani, Sicily, in 1659, and died at Naples October 24, 1725.

"O cessate di piagarmi" and "Se tu della mia morte" well exhibit his power of appealing to the feelings; and the arietta "Spesso vibra per suo giuoco" shows with what elegance he could write in the semi-serious vein.

DOMENICO SCARLATTI.
1685–1757.

THE son of Alessandro Scarlatti, some of whose graceful songs we have also printed, he was likewise his pupil, also studying under Gasparini. His fame was established while he was still a young man, and, as commonly the case in Italy at that period, by the performance of his operas; but for coming generations it is founded chiefly upon his unquestioned eminence as a player on and writer for the harpsichord. He also earned laurels as an organ-player, and at the time of Handel's visit to Rome (1709), was pitted against the latter by Cardinal Ottoboni. Among the multitude of his excellent compositions we note the curious *Fuga del gatto* (Cat-fugue), suggested by a cat's running across the keys of his harpsichord while he sat at work. Besides instrumental works he wrote not a few vocal compositions, among which may be mentioned several operas, a mass for four vocal parts and orchestra, a *Salve regina* with string-quartet, and some secular arias. Of these last the "Consolate e spera" strikes me as being remarkably attractive;—the movement is highly dramatical, and consequently the melody is certain to prove effective. It is also to be found in the collection of *Arien und Gesänge* noticed before.

In 1715 Scarlatti was appointed *maestro di cappella* at St. Peter's in Rome, which sufficiently shows the estimation in which he was held; he was also teacher of the harpsichord to the Princess of Asturia in Madrid from 1746 to 1754, then returning to Naples. His son Giuseppe was likewise a musician of note. Domenico was born at Naples in 1683, and died there in 1757 (or, according to other authorities, in Madrid).

TOMMASO TRAETTA.

1727-1779.

FROM the masterpiece of this composer, the *Antigone*, I have taken the scena and aria "Ombra cara, amorosa," the wondrous pleading of whose melodies and harmonies shows the height to which the great Italian composers of the 18th century carried the art of melodramatic expression. In the aria, as in the grand *scena* preceding it, the music seems wedded to the words; the *scena* has the broad form of an arioso, and is worthy of a place here as a model of its kind.

Traetta, a shining light of the Neapolitan school, was born at Bitonto, near Naples; for ten years (1738-1748) he studied under Durante, and his first opera, *Il Farnace*, which was brought out in 1750, met with remarkable favor, so that its fortunate author was immediately overwhelmed with orders from Italian theatres, in consequence of which he threw off opera after opera with almost careless haste. In 1758 he became music-director and court teacher at Parma, went to Venice in 1765, and three years later to St. Petersburg, where he stayed till 1776; thence he proceeded to London, where he met with a very cool reception, Sacchini being at that time the accepted favorite of court and public; he at length returned to Italy, and died on the 6th of April, 1779, at Venice.

ANTONIO VIVALDI.

16—(?)—1743.

ANTONIO VIVALDI, surnamed *il prete rosso* (the red priest) from the color of his hair, was born at Venice in the second half of the 17th century, and died there in 1743 as the Director of the *Conservatorio della Pietà*. He took holy orders while young, and became later a celebrated violinist and composer of dramatic and instrumental works. He wrote no less than twenty-eight operas, besides many trios, sonatas, and concertos for the violin and other instruments. The arietta "Un certo non so che" is a beautiful example of graceful expression and style, as well as of pleasing originality. Vivaldi held for some time a position as violinist at the court of the Elector Philip of Hesse-Darmstadt. The following curious anecdote is related of him:

While celebrating the mass one day, a sudden musical inspiration of such beauty seized him that he felt unable to let it go unnoticed; carried away by artistic enthusiasm, he stopped short in the midst of the holy office, retired into the sacristy, and wrote down the fugitive thought. Having done so, he quietly returned to the altar, and finished the interrupted mass. For this dereliction of duty he was summoned before the tribunal of the Holy Inquisition. Fortunately his judges, anticipating the modern theory of delinquency, pronounced him mad ; hence his punishment was limited to prohibiting him thenceforward from celebrating the mass.

CONTENTS

3
Vittoria, mio core!
(Victorious my heart is!)
Cantata.

English Version by
H. MILLARD.

GIAN GIACOMO CARISSIMI.
(1604(?)–1674)

Printed in the U.S.A.
Copyright, 1880, by G. Schirmer.

11105 a

sciolta_ d'A _ mo – re _ La _ vil ser vi – tù, È sciol – – –
love now has bro – ken its shackles in twain, For love_____

– – – – ta d'A – mo – re La ser – vi – tù.
now has bro – ken its shackles in twain.

meno mosso, e dolce assai.

Già l'em-pia a' tuoi dan – ni Fra stuo-lo di sguar-di, Con vez-zi bu-
The false one is vanquish'd, her glances a – muse me, De – ception no

giar-di Di – spo-se gl'in – gan – – ni; Le fro – de, gli af-
longer with arts can_ con – fuse_ me! No false-hood or

fan-ni Non han-no più lo - - co, Del cru - do suo fo - co È
sorrow op - press me with rig - - or, The flame, once so cru - el, has

f Tempo I.

spen-to _ l'ar - do - - - re! Vit - to - ria! Vit - to - ria! Vit-
spent all _ its _ vig - - - or! Vic - to - rious! Vic - to - rious! Vic-

p

to - ria! Vit - to - ria, mio co - - - re! Non la - grimar più, Non
torious! Vic - to - rious my heart is! And tears are in vain, And

la - gri-mar più, È sciol - ta d'A - mo - re La vil ser - vi -
tears are in vain, For love now has bro - ken its shack-les in

tù, È sciol - - - - - ta d'A-
twain, For love _____ now has

mo-re La ser - vi-tu! Da lu - ci ri - den-ti Non e-sce più
broken its shackles in twain! Her smile once en - trancing no darts is re-

meno mosso, e dolce assai.

strale, Che pia - ga mor-ta-le Nel pet-to m'av-ven - - ti: Nel
vealing, The wounds in my bo-som with time are all_ heal - -ing; All

duol,ne' tor-menti Io più non mi sfac - - cio E rot-to o-gni
sorrow and torment no lon-ger I'm fear - - ing, Now bro-ken each

Tempo I.

lac-cio, Spa - ri - to il ti - mo - - - re! Vit - to-ria! Vit - to-ria! Vit-
tie is, all fears dis - ap - pear - - - ing! Vic - to-rious, Vic - to-rious, Vic-

to-ria! Vit - to-ria, mio co - - - re! Non la - grimar più, Non la - grimar
torious, Vic - to-rious my heart is! And tears are in vain, And tears are in

più, È sciol - ta d'A - mo - re La vil ser - vi - tù, È sciol - -
vain, For love now has bro-ken its shackles in twain, For love _____

- ta d'A - mo-re La ser - vi - tù!
nowhas broken its shackles in twain!

Intorno all'idol mio.
(Caressing mine idol's pillow.)
Aria.

English Version by
Dr. TH. BAKER.

MARCO ANTONIO CESTI.
(1620 – 1669(?))

9

Che fiero costume.
(How void of compassion.)
Arietta.

English Version by
D! TH. BAKER.

GIOVANNI LEGRENZI.
(1625 _ 1690)

Allegretto con moto. (♪.= 56.)

Voice

Che fie - ro co - stu - me d'a - li - ge - ro nu - me, che a
How void of compas - sion Is Cu - pid his fashion, Who

Piano.

leggiero e grazioso

for - za di pe - ne si fac - cia a - do - rar, si fac - cia a - do - rar,____ che a
drives me by torment himself to a - dore, him - self to a - dore,____ Who

for - za di pe - ne si fac - cia a - do - rar!____
drives me by torment himself to a - dore!____

11107

cie - co bam - bi - no con boc - ca di lat - te si fac - cia sti - mar, si
boy so de - fence-less, Scarce wean'd, yet can make us his fa - vor im - plore, his

fac - cia sti - mar!_____ con boc - ca di lat - te si
fa - vor im - plore!_____ Scarce wean'd, yet can make us his

fac - cia sti - mar!
fa - vor im - plore!

Deh più a me non v'ascondete.
(Ah! why let me ever languish.)
Arietta.

English Version by
Dr. TH. BAKER.

GIOVANNI MARIA BONONCINI.
(1640 - 1703)

11108

sol, lu-ci va-ghe del mio sol, lu-ci va-ghe del mio sol.
Sun, In thy way-ward beams,my Sun, In thy way-ward beams,my Sun?

Con sve-lar-vi, se voi sie-te, voi po-te-te far que-st'al-ma fuor di duol, voi po-te-te far que-st'al-ma fuor di duol, far quest'al-ma fuor di duol.
Clear out-shin-ing, thou canst ban-ish All the anguish Of the night my soul doth shun, All the an-guish of the night my soul doth shun, of the night my soul doth shun.

Deh, più a me non v'a-scon-de-te, lu-ci va-ghe del mio
Ah why let me ev-er languish In thy waywardbeams,my

sol,   deh, più a me non v'a-scon-de-te, lu-ci va-ghe del mio
Sun?   Ah why let me ev-er languish In thy waywardbeams,my

sol,__ lu-ci va-ghe__del mio sol, lu-ci va-ghe del mio
Sun, in__ thy way-ward beams, my Sun, in thy way-ward beams, my

molto rit.

sol,__ lu-ci va-ghe__del mio__ sol.
Sun, in thy way-ward beams,my__ Sun?

col canto

p

ff

O cessate di piagarmi.

(O no longer seek to pain me.)

Arietta.

English Version by
Dr TH. BAKER.

ALESSANDRO SCARLATTI.
(1659 _ 1725)

Se Florindo è fedele.

(Should Florindo be faithful.)

Arietta.

English Version by
Dr. TH. BAKER.

ALESSANDRO SCARLATTI.
(1659 – 1725)

Allegretto grazioso, moderato assai. (♪= 132.)

io m'in - na - mo - re - rò.
I'll sure - ly, sure - ly fall in love.

Po - trà ben l'ar - co ten - de - re il fa - re -
How art - ful e'er he draw the bow, Well - vers'd in __

tra - to ar - cier, ch'io mi sa - prò di - fen - de - re d'un
arch - ers' wiles, My heart I can de - fend, I know, From

guar - do lu - sin - ghier. Pre - ghi,
a - ny lur - ing smiles. Sigh - ing,

Son tutta duolo.
(Desponding, lonely.)

Aria.

English Version by
Dr. TH. BAKER.

ALESSANDRO SCARLATTI.
(1659 - 1725)

Son tut - ta duo - lo,   non ho che affan - ni
Desponding, lone - ly   I here must lan - guish,

e mi dà mor - te pe - na cru - del, pe - na cru - del
Sore wounded e - ven For death I wait, for death I wait;

e mi dà mor - te pe - na cru - del, pe - na cru - del:
Sore wounded e - ven For death I wait, for death I wait;

Spesso vibra [31] per suo gioco.

(Oft the blindfold boy.)

Canzonetta.

English Version by
Dr. TH. BAKER.

ALESSANDRO SCARLATTI.
(1659 - 1725)

11112

gua - le que - sto man - - ca, que - - sto
sor - rows, None_____ so bold, no, none____ so

man - - ca e quel vien me - - no, que - - sto
cold,___ can play the sto - ic, none_____ so

man - ca, que - sto man - ca e quel vien me - no.
bold,___ no, none___ so cold__ can play the sto - ic.

Spes - so___ vi - bra per__ suo___
Oft___ the___ blind - fold boy___ doth___

Se tu della mia morte.

(Would'st thou the boast of ending.)

Aria.

English Version by
Dr. TH. BAKER.

ALESSANDRO SCARLATTI.
(1659 _ 1725)

Se tu____ del-la mia mor - te a que-sta de-stra
Would'st thou____ the boast of end - ing A life and love of-

for - te la glo-ria non vuoi dar, dal - la a'tuoi lu - mi, dal -
fend - ing De-ny to this right hand; Grant it to thine own eyes, grant

la a'tuoi lu _ mi.
it to thine own eyes.

Se tu del-la mia mor_te a
Would'st thou the boast of end-ing A

que_sta de _ stra for _ te la glo _ ria non vuoi dar,
life and love of - fend - ing De _ ny to this right hand,

dal - - - la,___ dal - la a'tuoi lu _ _ mi,
Grant it___ to thine, to thine own eyes,

dal - - - la,___ dal - la a'tuoi lu _ _ mi,
Grant it___ to thine, to thine own eyes;

rit. con grazia.

rit. col canto.

Un certo non so che.

(There's one, I know him not.)

Arietta.

English Version by
D.r TH. BAKER.

ANTONIO VIVALDI.
(16.... - 1743)

11114

Più sostenuto.

Un cer- to non so che,— un cer- to non so
There's one, I know him not,— there's one, I know him

che,— non so che— mi pas- sa il cor, e
not,— In- to my— heart did— rove, And

pur do - lor non è, e
yet no pain he brought, and

pur do - lor non è; mi giun-ge e pas- sa il
yet no pain he brought, in- to my heart did

Pur dicesti, o bocca bella.
(Mouth so charmful.)

Arietta.

English Version by
Dr. TH. BAKER.

ANTONIO LOTTI.
(1667_ 1740)

11115

che fa tut - to il mio pia - cer, _____ che _ fa tut - to il
That _ in thee all _ bliss is mine, _____ that _ in thee _ all

mio _ pia - cer, _____ il mio pia - cer.
bliss _ is _____ mine, _____ all bliss is _____ mine.

Per o -
E'en thy _

nor di sua fa - cel - la con un _ ba - cio A - mor t'a - prì, _
charms to vow com - pel me, Cu - pid _ ope'd thee with a kiss, _

11115

con un ba - cio A - mor t'a - prì,___ dol - ce
Cu - pid__ ope'd thee with__ a __ kiss,___ Thou sweet

fon - te__ del go - der, ah!_____ ah!
fount of joy di - vine, ah!_____ ah!

ah!_____ sì, del go - der.
ah!_____ fount of joy di - vine.

Tempo I.

Pur di -
Mouth so___

il mio pia - cer, quel _____ so - a - - ve e
all bliss is _____ mine, Why _____ thy sweet - ness

ca - - ro sì, sì, _____ che _____ fa tut - to il mio pia -
lures _____ me so, so, That _____ in thee all _____ bliss is

cer, _____ che fa tut - to il mio _____ pia - cer, _____ il
mine, _____ that in thee all bliss _____ is _____ mine, _____ all

mio pia - - cer.
bliss is _____ mine.

Sebben, crudele.
(Tho' not deserving.)
Canzonetta.

English Version by
Dr TH. BAKER.

ANTONIO CALDARA.
(1671 _ 1763)

rez - za sa - prò stan - car, la tua fie - rez - za
feel - ing I__ then shall move, Thy pride un - feel - ing

sa - prò stan - car.
I__ then shall__ move.

Seb - ben, cru - de - le, mi fai lan - guir,__
Tho' not de - serv - ing Thy cru - el scorn,__

sem - pre fe - de - le, sem - pre fe - de - le ti vo - glio a -
Ev - er un - swerv - ing, ev - er un - swerving Thee on - ly I__

mar.
love.

Seb - ben, cru -
Tho' not de -

f deciso.   p>   mf

cresc.   >   f

de - le,   mi fai lan - guir,____   sem - pre_ fe - de - le ti__
serv - ing   Thy cru - el   scorn,____   Ev - er_ un - swerv - ing Thee

rit assai.   mf   >   cresc.

vo - glio   a - mar,   seb - ben,   cru - de - le,   mi fai lan -
on - ly   I   love;   Tho' not   de - serv - ing   thy cru - el

rit assai.   mf   cresc.

f   >   >   rit assai.

guir,____   sem - pre_ fe - de - le ti_ vo - glio a - mar.____
scorn,____   Ev - er_ un - swerv - ing Thee on - ly I   love.____

f   rit assai.   pp

2 Ped.

Selve amiche, ombrose piante.
(Kindly forest.)

Arietta.

English Version by
D.ʳ TH. BAKER.

ANTONIO CALDARA.
(1671 - 1763)

11117

Come raggio di sol.

(As on the swelling wave.)

English Version by
D.ʳ TH. BAKER.

Aria.

ANTONIO CALDARA.
(1670 – 1763)

men - tre del ma - re, men - - tre del ma - re nel pro-
While in the bo - som, while___ in the bo - som of th'un-

fon - - do se - - no sta la tem - pe - -
fath - - om'd o - - cean There lies a tem -

- - - sta a sco - - - sa:
- - - pest in hid - - - ing:

co - sì ri - so ta - lor ga - io e pa - ca - to di con-
So are ma - - ny that wear a mien con - tent - ed, Ma-ny a

Consolati e spera!

(Take heart again!)

English Version by
Dr. TH. BAKER.

Aria.

DOMENICO SCARLATTI.
(1685 - 1757)

⁶⁹
Affanni del pensier.
(O agonies of thought.)
Arietta.

English Version by
Dr TH. BAKER.

GIORGIO FEDERICO HANDEL.
(1683 _ 1751)

fan - ni del __ pen - sier,　　　un　sol　mo - men - to
ag - o - nies __ of thought,　　　one　mo - ment on　 - 　ly

da-te-mi pa - ce almen, da-te-mi pa - ce almen, e
leave me in peace a-gain, leave me in peace a-gain, then

portando

poi tor-na - te. Af-fan-
turn and rend me. O ag-

- ni del pen-sier, un sol mo-men - to
- o-nies of thought, one mo-ment on - ly

da-te-mi pa-ce almen, e poi tor-na - te,
leave me in peace a-gain, then turn and rend me,

un sol mo - men - to   da - te - mi pa - ce al -
one mo - ment on - ly   leave me in peace a -

men,___ e poi tor - na - te,   tor - na - - -
gain,___ then turn and rend me,   one mo - - -

te,___ e poi tor - na - te;   Af - fan - ni del___ pen - sier,
ment, then turn and rend me;   O ag - o - nies___ of thought,

da - te - mi pa - ce almen,   e poi tor - na - te, e poi,___
leave me in peace a - gain   one moment on - ly, and then,___

Ah! mio cor.

(Ah, poor heart.)

Aria.

English Version by
Dr TH. BAKER.

GIORGIO FEDERICO HANDEL.
(1683 _ 1751)

11121

Ah! mio co - re, scherni - to se - i. Stel - le,___
Ah, poor heart! he scorns thy love. Hear me,___

De - i, Nu - me d'a - mo - re! tra - di -
Heaven, ye gods a - bove!___ Thee, O

to - re, t'a - mo tan - to, puoi la-sciar-mi sola in
trai-tor, love I on - ly, Canst thou leave me weeping,

pian - to, oh De - i, puo i la-
lone - ly, O Heav - en! canst___ thou___

sciar-mi so - la, so - la, so-la in pian - to,
leave me weeping, weeping, weeping, lone - ly,

Il mio bel foco.

(My joyful ardor.)

Recitativo ed Aria.

English Version by
D? TH. BAKER.

BENEDETTO MARCELLO.
(1686 _ 1739)

11122

Allegretto affettuoso.

Quella___ fiam-ma___ che m'ac- cen-de,
In my___ heart the___ flames that___ burn me,

quel-la___ fiam-ma___ che m'ac-
in my___ heart the___ flames that___

più f

cen-de   pia-ce tan-to all'al-ma   mi - a,   pia-ce tan-to all'al-ma
burn me   All my soul do so en - rav-ish,   all my soul do so en-

rit.
f portando

mi - a,   che giammai s'e-stin-gue - rà, s'e-stin-gue-rà, s'e-stin-gue-
ravish,   That they ne'er shall cease to   glow, shall cease to   glow, shall cease to

ren - de, va - ghi rai del mio bel so - le, al - tra luce el - la non
turn me, Wan - d'ring rays of my fair sun,__ Oth - er light I cov - et

vuo - le nè vo - ler giammai po - trà, nè vo -
none,_____ Nor the wish can ev - er know, nor the

cresc. poco a poco

ler__ giammai po - trà, nè vo - ler, nè vo - ler giam -
wish can ev - er know, nor the wish, nor the wish can__

cresc. poco a poco

mai po - trà, giammai po - trà,__ nè vo - ler giammai po -
ev - er__ know, can ev - er know,__ nor the__ wish can ev - er

col
canto

trà.
know.

a tempo   *cresc.*

Quel - la__ fiam - ma__ che m'ac - cen - de   pia - ce tanto al-l'al-ma
In my__ heart the__ flames that__ burn me   All my soul do so en -

mi - a,   pia - ce tanto al-l'al-ma   mi - a,   che giammai s'e-stin-gue-
ravish,   all my soul do so en - ravish   That they ne'er shall cease to

rit.   *mf*

rà, s'e - stin-gue - rà, s'e - stin-gue - rà,   pia - ce tanto al - l'al - ma
glow, shall cease to glow, shall cease to glow;   All my soul do so en -

f rit.

83

11122

84

Ogni pena più spietata.
(All of anguish most unsparing.)

English Version by
Dr. TH. BAKER.

Arietta.

GIOVANNI B. PERGOLESI.
(1710 _ 1736)

O - gni_ pe - na_ più spie - ta - ta, più spie - ta - ta
All of__ an - guish most un - spar - ing, most un - spar - ing

11123

pe - na_ più spie - ta - ta,_ più spie - ta - ta sof - fri -
an - guish most un - spar - ing, most un - spar - ing Fain would

ri - a que - st'al - ma af - flit - ta e de - so - là - ta, o - gni
bear this soul_ for - sak - en And _ de - spair - ing; all of

rit. *tratt.*

pe - na più spie - ta - ta sof - fri - ria quest'alma af - flit - ta, se go -
anguish most un - sparing Fain would bear this soul for - sak - en, If her

rit. *col canto.*

cresc. ed animando assai *f* *mf*

desse u - na spe - ran - za di po - ter - si con - so - lar._ ah,
hope remain'd un - shak - en To con - sole her - self once more._ ah,

cresc.

rar.
store.

Tempo I.

O - gni_ pe - na_ più spie - ta - ta,_ più spie -
All of_ an - guish most un - spar - ing,_ most un -

ta - ta sof - fri - ri - a que - st'al - ma af - flit - ta e
spar - ing Fain would bear_ this soul for - sak - en

de - so - la - ta, o - gni pe - na più spie - ta - ta sof - fri -
And _____ de - spair - ing, all of an - guish most un - spar - ing, Fain would

Stizzoso, mio stizzoso.

(Unruly, Sir, unruly?)

English Version by
D.^r TH. BAKER.

Aria.

GIOVANNI B. PERGOLESI
(1710 – 1736)

Voice. Piano.

Stiz - zo - so, mio stiz - zo - so, voi fa - te il bo - ri -
Un - ru - ly, Sir, un - ru - ly, And fain to play the

o - so, ma no, ma non vi può gio - va - re, ma
bul - ly? But naught, naught you'll gain by vio - lence, but

no, ma non vi può gio - va - re; bi - so - gna al mio di - vie - to star
naught, naught you'll gain by vio - lence; 'Tis time to end this ri - ot, Be

che — to, che — to; e non par - la - re,
qui - et, qui - et, And now keep si - lence,

zit_ zit_ Ser - pi - na_ vuol co - sì, zit_
hush! hush! Ser - pi - na_ you'll o - bey; hush!

zit_ Ser - pi - na_ vuol co - sì.
hush! Ser - pi - na_ you'll o - bey!

Stiz - zo - so, mio_ stiz -
Un - ru - ly, Sir,_ un -

zo - so, voi fa - te il bo - ri - o - so, ma no,
ru - ly, And fain to play the_ bul - ly? But naught,

ma non vi può gio - va - re; bi - so - gna al mio di - vie - to star
naught you'll gain by vio - lence; 'Tis time to end this ri - ot, Be

che - to, che - to; e non par - la - re,
qui - et, qui - et, And now keep si - lence;

zit_ zit_ Ser - pi - na_ vuol co - sì, voi
hush! hush! Ser - pi - na_ you'll o - bey. You

fa-te il bo - ri - o - so, ma non vi può gio - va - re, bi - sogna al mio di -
fain would play the bul-ly, But naught you'll gain by violence;'Tis time to end this

vie - to star che-to e non par - la - re, zit_ zit_
ri - ot; Be qui - et, and keep si - lence, hush! hush!

che - to, zit_ zit_ e non par - lar, Ser -
qui - et! hush! hush! keep si - lence now, Ser -

pi - na vuol co - sì, vuol co - sì, Ser - pi - na_
pi - na you'll o - bey, you'll o - bey, Ser- pi - na_

vuol co - sì. Cre -
you'll o - bey! I

d'io che m'in-ten-de-te, sì, che m'inten-de-te, sì, che m'inten-
think you com-pre-hend me, yes! you compre-hend me, yes! you compre-

de - te, da che mi co - no - sce - te son mol-ti e mol-ti dì, son
hend me, For you've not dared of - fend me This ma-ny and many a day, this

mol - ti, mol - ti e mol - ti dì.
ma - ny, ma - ny, this ma-ny a day.

Stiz - zo - so, mio — stiz -
Un - ru - ly, Sir, — un -

zo - so, voi fa - te il bo - ri - o - so, ma no,
ru - ly, And fain to play the — bul-ly? But naught,

ma non vi può gio - va - re; ma no, ma non vi può gio -
naught you'll gain by vio-lence, But naught, naught you'll gain by

va - re; bi - so - gna al mio di - vie-to star che — - to,
vio-lence;'Tis time to end this ri - ot; Be qui - - et,

che - - to; e non par - la - re, zit_ zit_
qui - - et; And now keep si - lence, hush! hush!

Ser-pi - na_ vuol co - sì, zit_ zit_ Ser-pi - na_
Ser-pi - na_you'll o - bey! hush! hush! Ser-pi - na_

vuol co - sì. Stiz-
you'll o - bey! Un-

zo - so, mio_stiz - zo-so, voi fa-te il bo - ri - o-so, ma
ru - ly, Sir,_un - ru-ly, And fain to play the_ bul-ly? But

no, ma non vi può gio - va - re: bi - so-gna al mio di - vie-to star
naught, naught you'll gain by vio-lence; 'Tis time to end this ri - ot; Be

che - to, che - to; e non par - la - re, zit_
qui - et, qui - et; And now keep si - lence; hush!

zit_ Ser-pi - na_vuol co - sì, voi fa-te il bo - ri - o-so, ma
hush! Ser-pi - na_you'll o - bey! You fain would play the bul-ly, But

non vi può gio-va-re, bi-sogna al mio di-vie-to star che-to e non par-
naught you'll gain by vio-lence; 'Tis time to end this ri-ot; Be qui-et, and keep

la - re, zit_ zit_ che - to, zit_ zit_
si - lence; hush! hush! qui - et! hush! hush!

e non par - lar. Ser-pi - na vuol co - sì, vuol co-
keep si - lence now. Ser-pi' - na wills it so, wills it

sì, Ser-pi - na _vuol co - sì.
so, Ser-pi - na _wills it so!

Se tu m'ami, se sospiri

(If thou lov'st me.)

Arietta.

English Version by
Dr. TH. BAKER.

GIOVANNI B. PERGOLESI.
(1710.—1736)

Se tu m'a - mi, se tu so-spi-ri Sol per me, gen-til pa - stor,—
Ho do-lor de' tuoi mar-ti-ri, Ho di-let-to del tuo a-mor, Ma se pen-si

If thou lov'st me, and sigh-est ev-er But for me, O gen-tle swain,
Sweet I find thy lov-ing fa-vor, Pi-ti-ful I feel thy pain. Shouldst thou think tho',

me, gen-til _ pa - stor, _ Ho do-lor de' tuoi mar-ti-ri, Ho di-let-to
me, O gen-tle _ swain, Sweet I find thy lov-ing fa-vor, Pi-ti-ful I

del tuo a-mor, Ma _ se-pen-si che so-let-to Io _ ti _ deb-ba ri - a-mar,
feel thy pain. Should'st thou think tho', that de-mure-ly I _ on thee a - lone _ may smile,

Pa-sto-rel - lo, sei sog-get-to Fa - cil-mente a t'in-gannar, Pa-sto-rel - lo,
Simple shepherd, thou art sure-ly Prone thy sens-es to beguile; Simple shepherd,

sei sog-get-to Fa - cil - mente a _ t'in-gannar, Fa - cil - mente a _ t'in-gannar:
thou art sure-ly Prone thy _ sens-es _ to beguile, prone thy _ sens-es _ to beguile.

O del mio dolce ardor.

(O thou belov'd.)

Aria.

English Version by
Dr. TH. BAKER.

CRISTOFORO GLUCK.
(1714 - 1787)

spi - - - - ro. Ah! ___ O del mio dol - ce ar -
fond - - - - er. Ah! ___ O thou be - lov'd whom

dor ___ bra - ma - to og-get - - to, bra-ma - to og-
long ___ my heart de - sir - eth, my heart de -

get - - - to, L'au - ra che tu re -
sir - - - eth, At length the air thou

Chi vuol comprar la bella calandrina.

(Who will buy the beautiful canary.)

English Version by
H. MILLARD.

NICCOLÒ JOMMELLI.
(1714–1774)

Allegretto grazioso. (♩ = 72)

Chi_ vuol com-prar la_ bel-la ca-lan-dri-_ -na, Che

Oh_ who will buy the_ beau-ti-ful ca-na-_ -ry, That

11105 b

can - ta da mat - ti - no in fi - no a se - ra? Chi _ vuol, chi _ vuol com -
sings from ear - ly morn to eve so gai - ly? Who wish - es _ now to

prar - la, ven - ga a con - trat - to! Ven - ga!
buy _ her? Come, make an of - fer! Come _ now!

ven - ga! Sempre a buon pat - to _ la _ ven - de -
come _ now! A bar - gain 'tis, such as _ ne'er _ was

rò, Sempre a buon pat - to _ la _ ven - de - rò. La
seen, a bar - gain 'tis, such as _ ne'er _ was seen. The

bel-la ca- lan- dri - - na! chi vuol, chi vuol com- prarla?
beauti-ful ca- na- - - ry! Who wish-es now to_ buy her?

chi? chi? Ven - ga! ven ga! Sem- pre a buon
Who? who? Come now! come now! A bar- gain

pat_ to_ la_ ven- de- rò, Sem-pre a buon pat- to_ la_ ven- de -
'tis, such as_ ne'er_ was seen, a bar- gain 'tis, such as_ ne'er_ was

ro. E_
seen. So_

sì gentil,ha_ co-sì dol-ce il can- -to, E ven-der la deg_
pretty,too, and sings so sweet and clear- -ly, Al -tno' I sell her,

g'io che l'a-mo tan-to; Ma que-sto è il mio me- stie -re, No'l fo per pia_
still I love her dear-ly; But 'tis to _earn a liv- -ing, Not for pleasure

ce-re! Ven-ga! ven-ga! Sempre a buon pat-to la_
striving! Come now, come now! A bargain 'tis, such as_

ven-de-rò, Sempre a buon pat-to la_ ven-de-rò. La
ne'er_was seen, a bar-gain 'tis, such as_ ne'er_was seen. The

bel-la ca_lan-dri — — na! chi vuol, chi vuol com - prarla?
beauti-ful ca - na - — ry! Who wish-es now to _ buy her?

chi? chi? Ven - ga! ven - ga! Sempre a buon
Who? who? Come now! come now! A bar-gain

pat - to_la _ ven - de - rò, Sempre a buon pat - to_la_ ven - de -
'tis, such as_ ne'er_was seen, a bar-gain 'tis, such as _ ne'er _ was

rò.
seen.

Ombra cara, amorosa.
(Gentle Shade, well beloved.)

Scena ed Aria.

English Version by
Dr. TH. BAKER.

TOMMASO TRAETTA.
(1727 - 1779)

Om - bra ca - ra a - mo - ro - sa, ah! per-chè ma - i tu
Gen - tle Shade, well be - lov - ed, ah, wherefore hast thou To

cor-ri al tuo ri - po - so, ___ ed io qui re - sto?
thy re-pose depart - ed, ___ and me for-sak - en?

Tu tran-
All the

quil - la godra - i nel - le se - di be - a - te, o - ve non
calm now enjoy - est thou Of th'a-bode of the bless - ed, where-to ex-

giun-ge nè sde-gno, nè do - lor; nè sde-gno, nè do - lor; do - ve ri-
tendeth Nor sor-row nor dis - tress, nor sor-row nor dis-tress; wherefrom are

co - pre o-gni cu-ra mor-ta-le e-ter-no ob-blì -
ban - ish'd All the cares of this earth, and ef-fac'd for ev-

cor-ri al tuo ri-po-so,___ ed io qui___ re - sto?
thy re-pose de-part-ed,___ and me for - sak - - en?

Andantino. (♩ = 108.)

Io re-sto sem-pre a pian-ge-re   do-ve mi gui-da o-
I still un-hap-py am wan-der-ing   Whith-er my fate may

gnor,   do - ve mi gui-da o - gnor
e'er,   Whith-er my fate may   e'er

d'un in un al - tro o - ror,
Deep- er in dark   de - spair.

O notte, o Dea del mistero.

(O night, mysterious Goddess.)

Aria.

English Version by
Dr. TH. BAKER.

NICCOLÒ PICCINNI.
(1728 - 1800)

nuit,— — — — -te, Dé - es - se du— mys - tè - re,
not- — — — — -te, o De - a del— mi - ste - ro,
night,— — — — — mys - te - rious God - dess lone - ly,

11128

dou - ce com - pa - gne de l'a - mour,
dol - ce com - pa - gna d'a - mor;
Love's dear com - pan - ion and friend,

nuit,_____ c'est en toi que j'es - pè - re!
not - - te, è in te so - la ch'io spe - ro!
night,_____ I can hope in thee on - ly!

hâ - te - toi_____ de chas - ser_ le
deh_ scac - - cia del gior - no il ful -
Haste, O hast - - en, that day_ do

jour;_
gor;_
end;_

hâ - te - toi_____
deh_ scac - -
Haste, O hast - - -

11128

Chi vuol la zingarella.

(Who'll try the Gipsy pretty.)

Canzone.

English Version by
D.ʳ TH. BAKER.

GIOVANNI PAISIELLO.
(1741 _ 1816)

Chi   vuol la zin-ga-
Who'll   try the Gip-sy

rel-la   gra - ziosa ac-corta e   bel-la?   Si - gnori, ec-co-la_ qua,   si-
pretty,   So winning, wise and   wit-ty,   As_ one and all may see,   As

gnori, ec-co - la qua.
one and all may see?

Le don-ne sul bal - co - ne
For la-dies at their win - dow

so bene in-do-vi - nar.
Their fortune I can tell;

I giovani al can -to - ne
The laddies at the inn,— too,

so meglio stuzzi - car.
I can amuse as well.

A— vecchi in-na-mo-ra-ti scal - dar fo— le cer-
When old men feel love burning, I— set their heads a -

vel-la, scal - dar fo— le cér-vel-la, a— vecchi inna-mo-ra - ti. Chi
turning, I— set their heads a - turn-ing, When old men feel love burn - ing. Who'll

vuol la zin-ga - rel-la, chi vuol la zin-ga - rel-la? Si - gnori, ec-co-la—
try the Gip-sy pretty, Who'll try the Gip-sy pretty? Come one and all to—

vuol la zin-ga-rel-la gra - zio-sa, ac-cor-ta e
try the Gip-sy pret-ty, So win-ning, wise and

bel-la? Si - gno-ri, ec-co-la qua; si-
wit-ty, As one and all may see, as

gno-ri, ec-co-la qua, gra-zi-o-sa, ac-cor-ta e
one and all may see; So win-ning, wise and

bel-la, gra-zi-o-sa, accor-ta e bel - la. Si-gno-ri, ec-co-la
wit-ty, so winning, wise and wit - ty, As one and all may

Nel cor più non mi sento.

(Why feels my heart so dormant.)

Arietta.

English Version by
Dr. TH. BAKER.

GIOVANNI PAISIELLO.
(1741 _ 1816)

Nel cor più non mi sen - to bril - lar la _ gio - ven -
Why feels my heart so dor - mant No fire of _ youth di -

tù; ca - gion del mio _ tor - men - to, a -
vine? Thou cause of all _ my tor - ment, O

mor, sei col - pa tu. Mi piz - zi - chi, mi stuz - zi - chi, mi
Love, the fault __ is thine! He teas - es me, he pinches me, He

pun - gi - chi, mi mas - ti - chi; che co - sa è que - sto ahi - mè? __ pie -
squeezes me, he wrenches me; What tortures I __ must bear! Have

tà, pie - tà, pie - tà! a - mo - re è un cer - to che, __ che
done, have done, have done! Thou, Love, art sure - ly one __ Will

di - spe - rar __ mi fa.
drive me to __ de - spair!

Il mio ben quando verrà.

(When, my love, wilt thou return.)

English Version by
Dr. TH. BAKER.

Aria.

GIOVANNI PAISIELLO.
(1741-1816)

Il mi - o ben   quan - do   ver - rà
When,   my love,   wilt thou re - turn,

a ___ ve - der   la __ me - sta a - mi - ca?
Her ___ to see   for __ thee who is sigh - ing?

dol - - ci, più dol - - ci ac - cen - - ti.
gen - - tly, more gen - -tly re - ply - - ing.

Ma non l'o - do.
Who can hear him?

E chi l'u - dì?
No voice hear I!

Ah! il mio be - ne am - mu - to - lì.
Ah! still my lov - er makes no re - ply.

Ah! am - mu - to - lì.
Ah! makes no re - ply.

Plaisir d'amour.

(The Joys of Love.)

English Version by
H. MILLARD.

GIOVANNI MARTINI.
(1741 _ 1816)

11105 c

mour du-re tou-te la vi - - - - - - e.
mor tut-ta la vi-ta du - - - - - ra.
bit - ter thro'_ a life - time _____ prove.

J'ai tout quit -
Tut-to scor-dai per
I gave up per

té pour l'in - gra-te Syl - vi - - - e; _____
le - i, per Sil-via in - fi - - - da; _____
all_ for cru - el Syl - via's _____ love, _____

el - - le me quit-te et prend un au - - tre a -
el - la_or mi scor-da_e_ad al - tro a - mor s'af - fi -
Too soon I find an - oth - er owns her _____

"Tant que cet-te eau - cou - le - ra dou - ce - ment _____ vers
"Fin - chè tran-quil - lo scor - re - rà il ru - scel _____ là
"Long as this brook - let shall soft - ly on - ward flow, _____ The

dolce.

ce ruisseau qui bor - de la _ prai - ri - e je t'ai - me
ver - so il mar che cin - ge la _ pia - nu - ra io t'a - me
mead - ow pass - ing on _ its joy - ous way, _____ Thee I _ will

cresc.

rai," me ré - pé - tait _ Syl - vi - e.
rò," mi dis - se l'in - fe - de - le.
love," ev - er would Syl - via say: _____

L'eau _____ cou - le en - cor, el - le a chan - gé _____ pour _
Scor - re il ri - o an - cor, ma can - giò in lei _____ l'a -
Still _____ flows the stream, _____ but chang'd is Syl - via

SCHIRMER'S LIBRARY
of Musical Classics
VOCAL STUDIES AND EXERCISES
SERIES ONE

The Library Volume Number is given in brackets: [453]

ABT, F.
Op. 474. **Practical Singing Tutor.** For all Voices (Spicker).
For Soprano or Tenor. Complete [453] 2.00
  Part I: Production of Tone. Intervals [454] .75
  Part II: Exercises for the Cultivation of Fluency [455] .75
  Part III: 20 Solfeggi [456] .75
  Part IV: 12 Exercises on Vocalization [457] .75
For Mezzo-Soprano or Alto. Complete [458]. 2.00
  Part I: Production of Tone. Intervals [459] .75
  Part II: Exercises for the Cultivation of Fluency [460] .75
  Part III: 20 Solfeggi [461] .75
  Part IV: 12 Exercises on Vocalization [462] .75
For Baritone or Bass. Complete [463] 2.00
  Part I: Production of Tone. Intervals [464] .75
  Part II: Exercises for the Cultivation of Fluency [465] .75
  Part III: Solfeggi and Exercises on Vocalization [466] .75

BEHNKE, E, & PEARCE, C. W.
30 Voice-Training Exercises.
  For Soprano [1090] 1.25
  For Mezzo-Soprano [1091] 1.25
  For Alto [1092] 1.25
  For Tenor [1093] 1.25
  For Baritone [1094] 1.25
  For Bass [1095] 1.25

BONA, P.
Rhythmical Articulation. A Complete Method [1170] 1.00

BONOLDI, F.
Exercises in Vocalization.
Sop. [117]; M.-Sop. [118]; Alto [119] .75

BORDOGNI, M.
25 Easy Vocalises in Progressive Order [82].. 1.00
36 Vocalises in Modern Style (Spicker)
  For Soprano [432] 2.50
  For Mezzo-Soprano or Baritone [433] 2.50

CONCONE, J.
Op. 9. **50 Lessons.** H [1468]; M [242]; L [243] 1.25
Op. 10. **25 Lessons.** M [244]; L [246] 1.00

CONCONE, J.—*Continued*
Op. 11. **30 Daily Exercises.** H [294]; L [555] . 1.00
Op. 12. **15 Vocalises.** Finishing Studies. H [275]; M or L [276] 1.00
Op. 17. **40 Lessons.** Alto [247]; Bass or Bar. [248] 1.50
The School of Sight-Singing. Practical Method for Young Beginners (Lütgen) [245].. 1.25

DANNHÄUSER, A. L.
Solfège des Solfèges.
  Bk. I [1289]; Bk. II [1290]; Bk. III [1291].ea. 1.00
  The same. sp. Bk. I [1085] 1.00

ESLAVA, D. H.
Método de Solféo (Carrillo). sp. Complete [1366] 1.50
  The same. Bk. I [1376]; Bk. II [1377]; Bk. III [1378]; Bk. IV [1379] ea. .60

LAMPERTI, F.
The Art of Singing [1587] 1.00
Daily Exercises in Singing [570] .75
Vocal Studies in Bravura (Liebling) [1633] 1.00

LAMPERTI, G. B.
30 Preparatory Vocalises. Sop. [568] 1.25
29 Preparatory Vocalises. Alto [569] 1.25

LÜTGEN, B.
Vocalises (Spicker).
  Bk. I: 20 Daily Exercises. H [654]; M [655]; L [656] .75
  Bk. II: 20 Operatic Vocalises. M [930]; .75

MARCHESI, M. C.
Op. 1. **Elementary Progressive Exercises** [384] 1.00
Op. 2. **24 Vocalises for Soprano or Mezzo-Soprano** [391] 1.00
Op. 3. **24 Vocalises for Soprano** [597] 1.50
Op. 21. **The Art of Singing.** Bk. I: Elementary and Graduated Exercises [793]; Bk. II: 30 Vocalises for Mezzo-Soprano [794] ea. 1.00
Op. 32. **30 Vocalises** (Liebling) H or M [126]. 1.25

(Languages of texts are shown in small letters: e.=English; i.=Italian; sp.=Spanish. Where there is no other indication, texts are in English only. Other abbreviations used: H=High; M=Medium; L=Low; Bar.=Baritone; M.-Sop.=Mezzo-Soprano; Sop.=Soprano; Ten.=Tenor.)

Any Schirmer Library volume may be obtained in cloth binding. Prices will be quoted on request.
Prices Subject to Change Without Notice.

G. SCHIRMER, INC.   NEW YORK